Terms and Conditions

LEGAL NOTICE

(BLP13042016)

The Publisher has strived to be as accurate and complete as possible in the creation of this report, notwithstanding the fact that he does not warrant or represent at any time that the contents within are accurate due to the rapidly changing nature of the Internet.

While all attempts have been made to verify information provided in this publication, the Publisher assumes no responsibility for errors, omissions, or contrary interpretation of the subject matter herein. Any perceived slights of specific persons, peoples, or organizations are unintentional.

JUST JUICE By Danielle James

JUST JUICE

For Instant Weight Loss
and
Vibrant Vitality

By

Danielle James

GET THIS FREE EBOOK
UNLEASH your LEANER NEW YOU Right Now
Just search it over the internet

Table of Contents

Foreword

Whether it is just a fad or an exercise that is here to stay, juicing is becoming more and more popular, especially for those who are very health conscious. However in order to get the best benefits out of the juicing exercise some points should be taken into careful consideration. Get all the info you need here.

Get Juiced!

Juicing your way to better health

JUST JUICE By Danielle James

Chapter 1:

Get Started With Healthy Juicing

Synopsis

Juicing can be incorporated into the daily lifestyle for the purpose of enhancing healthy living and it is also a good way on increasing the daily intake of fruits and vegetables.

The Basics

For most people though juicing is either a chore and a bother or a welcomed alternative, however for those who enjoy juicing it is greatly encouraged as its better to do it personally than to buy juice products.

All juice products have to be treated and processed to ensure its integrity and shelf life, therefore homemade juices are a better choice to make.

However when doing homemade juices, it should be noted that it is very important to consume the juice product as soon as it is ready as letting it sit will only encourage the growth of pathogens and they also tend to break down faster when exposed to air, thus effectively losing a lot of its originally touted value.

It should also be noted that although consuming juices as a regular habit, limiting the juicing to only fresh fruits would not be a very good idea as a lot of fruits have a naturally high sugar content and are not so high in fiber, thus causing the negative build up of sugar levers in the body system. This may lead to diabetic and weight gain issues. A better alternative would be to combine complimenting fruits and vegetables together to form one delicious concoction that is both tasty and healthy. Accompanying this with a healthy fat and lean protein diet is also an added advantage.

Chapter 2:

Benefits of Healthy Juicing

Synopsis

As more people indulge in this form of healthy nutritional intake, it is becoming more popular to consume fruits and vegetable through juicing rather than eating these items as a whole and in its original form.

However scientist and nutritionist are or two minds when it comes to the merits of juicing as opposed to consuming these items whole, although there is yet to be any proven data to merit or advocate either choice over the other.

Advantages

There should however be some knowledge on the matter, before actually making juicing a permanent feature in an individual's lifestyle.

Studies have shown that juicing is one way of getting all the fruits and vegetable requirements into the body system effectively though albeit without the positive addition of the fiber needs.

It is arguably a more effective way of getting the nutrients adsorbed into the body system without putting undue pressure on the digestive system to break down the fibers.

For those who naturally have a dislike for consuming fruits and vegetable, juicing may present a more acceptable alternative.

There are also a variety of recipes available to make the juicing concoctions more agreeable and even tasty. Juicing combinations of vegetables and fruits are good to include in the recipe sourcing exercise.

Most juicing recipes include the parts of the fruits that would otherwise be discarded in the more conventional way of consuming them.

However with juicing the inclusion of pits, peelings, seeds and other parts are usually all included in the process for it has been noted that these contain a rich source of vital nutrients which are usually systematically thrown out.

Processed juices usually require some heating process to enhance the shelf life of the product and this can cause the enzymes to be killed. However with juicing this can be avoided and the enzyme content can be kept intact.

JUST JUICE By Danielle James

Chapter 3:

Healthy Juice Recipes

Synopsis

There are a lot of positive reasons that eventually encourage more people to juicing and this may include the ability to save cash due to the fact that the fruits can be bought in bulk, the definite benefits it can bring to controlling weight gain and shrinking the waist line, creating a fulfilling and healthy diet plan and increasing the energy and vitality levels in an individual.

JUST JUICE By Danielle James

Recipes

The following are some of the more popular juice recipes for the avid juicer:

Lemony apple – 2 apples, 1 lemon, 1" slice of ginger. This is a healthy remedy for colds as it is rich in flavonoid content. It also has a fresh and tangy taste that is quite invigorating.

Alkaline juice – 1 cup of spinach, ½ cup of cucumber, 2 stalks of celery including the leaves. 3 carrots and ½ an apple. The skin of the dark green cucumber will provide the source of chlorophyll which is a phytochemical that can help to build up the red blood cells. The cucumbers also contain silica which is a mineral that is good for the skin.

A Very Berry Medley – 2 cups of strawberries, 2 cups of blueberries and 1.5 cups of raspberries. Berries are a popular choice for juicing due to its quick and easy breakdown process and its simple rinse action. Being a great source of antioxidants such as anthocyanins, flavonoid and ellagic acid all or which have good anti cancer and anti heart diseases benefits.

Pomegranate juice – 5 pomegranates. In this recipe only the seeds are used and the rest of the fruit is discarded. However some may find better results using a blender as the seed does present a challenge to break down.

1. Perfect Pear Green Protein

Ingredients
1 packet (2 scoops) DailyBurn Fuel-6 Protein in vanilla
1 cup unsweetened almond milk
1 cup spinach
1 pear, cored
1/2 teaspoon of matcha tea powder

Directions
Combine all ingredients in a blender and mix until smooth.

2. Orange Kale Bonanza

Ingredients
1 packet (2 scoops) DailyBurn Fuel-6 Protein in vanilla
1 cup water
1 cup raw chopped kale
1 orange, peel and seeds removed
1/2 teaspoon of spirulina powder
1 pinch of ground cinnamon
1 pinch of ginger powder

Directions
Combine all ingredients in a blender and mix until smooth.

3. Ginger-Orange Green Perfection

Ingredients
1 ½ cups filtered water
4 generous handfuls fresh spinach
4 romaine leaves (optional)
2 navel oranges
2 ripe bananas
1"-2" knob of fresh ginger
1 cucumber (optional) peel if not organic

Directions
Rinse and prep veggies.
If you have a high-powered blender, throw everything in and blend until smooth.
If not, first blend the spinach and romaine until smooth, then add the remaining ingredients and blend.
Pour into a glass (so you can see the beautiful color) and enjoy!

4. Blueberry Mint Mouthful

Ingredients

2 cups spinach (These will blend better if you freeze them beforehand)

2 cups blueberry (I used 1 c. fresh and 1 c. frozen)

1 kiwi

3-4 large mint leaves

1 cup coconut water

1 cup ice

Directions

Put all ingredients in a blender and mix it up!

5. Sexy Spring Detox

Ingredients
1 cup green tea, chilled
1 cup loosely packed cilantro
1 cup loosely packed organic baby kale (or another baby green)
1 cup cucumber
1 cup pineapple
juice of 1 lemon
1 tablespoon fresh ginger, grated
½ avocado

Directions
Place ingredients into a blender and puree until smooth.

6. Gorgeous Green

Ingredients
1/2 banana
3/4 cup milk
2 big handfuls spinach
1/4 cup raw rolled oats
1/2 scoop Vega Choc-a-Lot
1 tbsp flax
Ancient Granola topping

Directions
Place ingredients into a blender and puree until smooth.

7. Sweet Melon

Ingredients
1/2 honeydew melon, cut into chunks (about 4 cups, or 1 1/2 lbs)
1/2 cup light coconut milk
1-2 leaves fresh mint (plus more for garnish)
1/2-1 tsp. fresh lime juice (or to taste)
1 cup ice
Drizzle of honey or coconut nectar, to taste (optional, depending on how sweet your melon is)

Directions
Cut your melon in half, remove the seeds, and slice away the outer rind. Cut the melon into chunks, and add to your blender along with the coconut milk, mint, lime, and ice. Blend until smooth. Taste, and adjust sweetness with honey or coconut nectar. Serve with a garnish of mint, or fresh melon slices.

8. Peachy Green

Ingredients

2 scoops Daily Burn Fuel-6 in vanilla

1 cup unsweetened almond milk

1 cup frozen peaches

1/2 cup frozen pineapple

1/2 banana

2 cups kale

1 tablespoon ground flaxseed

Preparation

Add all ingredients to blender. Mix until smooth.

9. Kale piña

Good for 2
Serving Size: 12 oz

Ingredients
2/3 c unsweetened vanilla almond milk
2 large hand-fulls (~50 g) kale ~the leaves of about 8 stalks
1/3 c (~80 g) pineapple chunks
1/2 (~50 g) ripe avocado
1 scoop protein powder (i used vanilla)
1 c ice cubes

instructions
put all ingredients into a blender and puree until smooth!

10.   Almond Peanut

Ingredients
3/4 cup almond milk
1/4 cup strong espresso, slightly cooled
1/2 cup frozen banana
1/4 cup smooth peanut butter
1/4 cup dark chocolate, roughly chopped
ice, as needed
agave syrup, optional to sweeten

Directions
 Pour milk and espresso into blender jar. Add frozen banana and peanut butter. Add about a half a cup of ice. Cover with lid and press auto smoothie button. Taste smoothie and add agave syrup as needed to sweeten. Add additional ice if thicker consistency is desired. Add chopped dark chocolate and pulse for a couple seconds until chocolate bits are distributed (and added ice is blended).
 Remove blender from machine, open spout and pour into 2 glasses. Serve immediately. Garnish with a banana slice and additional chocolate chunks.

11.   Wake up to Perfection

Ingredients
2 cups romaine lettuce (about 6 leaves) or baby spinach
1 cups tomato (about 1 tomato)
1 cup coconut water or filtered water (use water if on Body Ecology diet)
1 cup chopped carrot (about 1 carrot)
1 whole cucumber
1 avocado
1 whole lime peeled
2 garlic cloves
½ tsp Celtic sea salt
pinch of cayenne pepper
some ice cubes

Directions
Put all of the ingredients in your blender and puree until smooth and creamy.
Adjust salt quantities to taste.
Enjoy your daily dose of veggies for the day. YUMMO!
Serves 2.

12.   The Detox Delight

Ingredients
¾ cup (180 mL) filtered water
2 big red apples, diced
1 cup (30g) baby spinach
1" (2.5 cm) piece of fresh ginger, peeled and diced
1 teaspoon flax oil (optional)
1/2 teaspoon wheatgrass powder (optional)
tiny pinch cayenne pepper (optional)
1 cup ice cubes

Directions
Throw all of the ingredients into your high-speed blender and blast for 30 to 60 seconds until well combined. Enjoy right away while still fresh, and give a little stir if separation occurs.

13.   **Pumpkin Pie Perfection**

Ingredients
2 cups filtered water
1/2 cup raw, unsalted cashews, soaked
1/4 cup rolled oats
1 cup canned or freshly mashed pumpkin
1 fresh or frozen ripe banana
2 tablespoons maple syrup, plus or more to taste
1 teaspoon natural vanilla extract
1 1/4 teaspoons ground cinnamon, plus more to taste
1/2 teaspoon ground ginger, plus more to taste
1/4 teaspoon ground nutmeg, plus more to taste
tiny pinch ground cloves
pinch of Celtic sea salt
1 cup ice cubes

Directions:
Throw all the ingredients (except the ice into the blender and blast on high for 30 to 60 seconds until smooth and creamy.
Add the ice and blast again for about 10 seconds until chilled.

14.   Rose Melon

Ingredients

3 cups (480g) chopped seedless watermelon, chilled

1 teaspoon finely grated lemon zest

1 lemon, peeled and seeded

1 1/2 teaspoons finely chopped rosemary

1/2 cup (80g) frozen pineapple

1/4 cup (80g) frozen strawberries

5 drops alcohol-free liquid stevia, plus more to taste (optional)

Optional Boosters

1/2 cup (60g) frozen raw cauliflower florets

1/2 teaspoon cold-pressed, extra-virgin olive oil

1/4 teaspoon finely chopped jalapeño chile

Directions

Throw all of the ingredients into your Vitamix and blast on high for 30 to 60 seconds, until well combined.

15.   Carrot Pecan

Ingredients

3 cups filtered water

4 tablespoons sprouted or raw pecan butter or 1 1/4 cups soaked raw pecans

2 medium organic carrots - tops removed, peeled, and chopped

1 1/2 teaspoons ground cinnamon

1 crushed cardamom pod or 1/4 teaspoon cardamom powder

2 teaspoons natural vanilla extract

2 tablespoons maple syrup or 2 soft pitted dates, or stevia to taste

Directions

Throw all of the ingredients into your Vitamix and blast on high for about 1 minute until smooth and creamy. Taste and tweak sweetener to your preference.

Strain with a nut milk bag or fine mesh sieve to remove the pulp.

Enjoy this as a drink or use as a base in smoothies.

This will keep chilled in the fridge for 2 to 3 days covered.

16.   Winter Wonderland

Ingredients
1/2 cup frozen blueberries
1/2 avocado
1/2 small frozen banana
1 handful baby spinach (or kale)
2 cups water
1 tbsp cocoa powder
1 tbsp raw honey
Pinch of cayenne

Directions
Throw all of the ingredients into your high-speed blender and blast for 30 to 60 seconds until well combined. Enjoy right away while still fresh, and give a little stir if separation occurs.

17.   Carrot Cinnamon

Ingredients:

2 medium carrots, peeled and chopped

1/2 frozen banana

2 cups spinach

1 cup unsweetened soy milk

1/2 scoop vanilla protein powder (I used Vega Performance Protein)

1/8 cup golden raisins

1/2 teaspoon cinnamon

Dash of ground nutmeg

Dash of ground cloves

3 ice cubes

Directions

Throw all of the ingredients into your high-speed blender and blast for 30 to 60 seconds until well combined. Enjoy right away while still fresh, and give a little stir if separation occurs.

18.   Arthritis Assistance

Ingredients
Peeled and cut fresh pineapple chunks of one medium size pineapple
1 green cardamom
1 inch fresh ginger (peeled and cut)

Directions
Blend or juice all the above in a slow juicer and enjoy a different flavour and taste.
Cardamom is a spice and may be found in Asian markets if not available from your local grocery.

19. Skinny Cruiser

Ingredients
8 celery stalks
2 medium cucumbers or equivalent
½ bunch parsley
1 small lemon (I prefer Meyer lemons)

Directions
Throw all of the ingredients into your high-speed blender and blast for 30 to 60 seconds until well combined. Enjoy right away while still fresh, and give a little stir if separation occurs.

20.   Liver Detox

Ingredients
Pour some Aloe Vera Juice in the jar then add the juice of:
1 stalk Celery
1 carrot
1 apple
handful dandelion
handful parsley
¼ red cabbage
and fresh ginger root

Directions
Throw all of the ingredients into your high-speed blender and blast for 30 to 60 seconds until well combined. Enjoy right away while still fresh, and give a little stir if separation occurs.
Drink up and cleanse your liver.

***note** Fresh gel from the aloe leaf is best for this drink.

21.   Wild Greens Bonanza

Ingredients
1½ pounds of fresh wild greens
½ hothouse cucumber
6 celery tops
3 to 4 stalks of bok choy
1 whole lemon
1" chunk of fresh ginger root
miner's lettuce
chick weed
dandelion
sow thistle
yellow dock

Directions
Throw all of the ingredients into your high-speed blender and blast for 30 to 60 seconds until well combined. Enjoy right away while still fresh, and give a little stir if separation occurs.

22.   Red Starter

Ingredients
1 beet
1 cup red cabbage
2 carrots
1/2 sweet red pepper
1 orange peeled
1 apple
1 inch ginger

Directions
Throw all of the ingredients into your high-speed blender and blast for 30 to 60 seconds until well combined. Enjoy right away while still fresh, and give a little stir if separation occurs.

23.   Daily Detox Delight

Ingredients

1 cup greens (kale, chard, spinach, romaine, beet greens, or a combination)

1 cup green or red cabbage

1 cup napa cabbage

1 Granny Smith apple

4 stalks celery

4 carrots

3 red or golden beets (or a combination)

1 large cucumber

1 lemon

1 lime

2 bell peppers (any color)

1-2 inch piece of ginger root

Directions

Throw all of the ingredients into your high-speed blender and blast for 30 to 60 seconds until well combined. Enjoy right away while still fresh, and give a little stir if separation occurs.

Make sure all the veggies are washed and scrubbed, don't bother peeling anything, cut the apple down to the size your juicer will tolerate, juice lemon and lime WITH PEEL

24.   Fast and Furious

Ingredients

3 Whole bunches of Kale

20 Stalks of celery

2 Inch of ginger

5 lb bag of gala apple/Fuji (skin on, no seeds/stem)

1 Carton of Strawberries

1 lb Carrots

4 Bunches baby spinach

2 English cucumbers

1 lemon

1 pineapple (Rind Removed)

5 pears

1/2 cabbage

Directions

Throw all of the ingredients into your high-speed blender and blast for 30 to 60 seconds until well combined. Enjoy right away while still fresh, and give a little stir if separation occurs.

25.   Hair Helper

Ingredients
1 aloe vera leaf
1 cucumber
3 stalks of kale
½ onion
3 carrots

Directions
Throw all of the ingredients into your high-speed blender and blast for 30 to 60 seconds until well combined. Enjoy right away while still fresh, and give a little stir if separation occurs.

26. Sweet Sensation

Ingredients for Sweet Tart
2-3 golden beet roots (no leaves)
6 carrots
3 large pink grapefruit
1 green apple
2" ginger root
1 lemon, no peel

Directions
Throw all of the ingredients into your high-speed blender and blast for 30 to 60 seconds until well combined. Enjoy right away while still fresh, and give a little stir if separation occurs.

27.   Better Beet

Ingredients of Holiday Beet Juice
1 beetroot
4 to 5 carrots
3 to 4 celery stalks
Handful of cilantro
½ lime, with peel
1" chunk of fresh ginger root, or more to taste

Directions
Throw all of the ingredients into your high-speed blender and blast for 30 to 60 seconds until well combined. Enjoy right away while still fresh, and give a little stir if separation occurs.

28.   Winter Wonderland

Ingredients for Winter Brew Juice
5 - 6 carrots
5 – 6 stalks of celery
1 beetroot
Handful of parsley
½ bunch of kale
1" chunk of fresh ginger root, or more to taste

Optional:
½ lemon, peel and all
Cucumber

Directions
Throw all of the ingredients into your high-speed blender and blast for 30 to 60 seconds until well combined. Enjoy right away while still fresh, and give a little stir if separation occurs.

29.   Anti Diabetes

Ingredients
2 Baby cucumbers
2 Tomatoes
½ Bitter melon

Directions
Extract the juice of the above three, through a slow juicer, like Omega or Hurom.
This is very good for diabetes.

30.   Beautiful Broccoli

Ingredients
1 head of broccoli
2 carrots
2 handfuls of spinach
1 red apple

Directions
Throw all of the ingredients into your high-speed blender and blast for 30 to 60 seconds until well combined. Enjoy right away while still fresh, and give a little stir if separation occurs.

This juice tasted sweet and with all the greens it had the benefits our bodies need.

31.   Amazing Apple Flavor

Ingredients
Kale
Spinach
Celery
Fuji apple
1 tablespoon chia seeds (optional)

Directions
Throw all of the ingredients into your high-speed blender and blast for 30 to 60 seconds until well combined. Enjoy right away while still fresh, and give a little stir if separation occurs.
serve over ice if you like
Stir in the chia seeds to thicken up the juice and make a more sustaining snack or meal out of it.

32.   Peachy Green

Ingredients

1 head iceberg lettuce (you could use any variety of lettuce, but iceberg works well)

1/2 head green cabbage

1 inch square of fennel bulb (be generous)

2 inches ginger root (again, be generous)

4 peaches (remove the pit!)

10 grapes-green if you can, but any will do

Directions

Throw all of the ingredients into your high-speed blender and blast for 30 to 60 seconds until well combined. Enjoy right away while still fresh, and give a little stir if separation occurs.

33.   Sunset Sensation

Ingredients
3 Large Celery Stalks
2 Large Carrots
1 Dessert Pear
1 Medium Apple
1 Lemon Peel On
1/4 Honeydew Lemon
1/4 Small Pineapple
1" Root Ginger (optional)

Directions
Throw all of the ingredients into your high-speed blender and blast for 30 to 60 seconds until well combined. Enjoy right away while still fresh, and give a little stir if separation occurs.

34.   Spicy Veggie

Ingredients
My favorite juice, which I created. It's warming on a cold winter's day.
3 large juicy tomatos
2 carrots
1 large red chili
1 hand full of coriander (also known as cilantro) leaves and stalks

Directions
Juice all of the above ingredients and then give the juice a good stir. This juice is lovely if you make and put it in the fridge and drink it really cold.

35.   Cool Cucumber Kiwi

Ingredients
2 Kiwis
1/2 Cucumber
5 Strawberries
1 Celery Rib
2-3 Kale Leaves
Handful of Dandelion greens or Spinach
1 Apple
1 Carrot

Directions
Throw all of the ingredients into your high-speed blender and blast for 30 to 60 seconds until well combined. Enjoy right away while still fresh, and give a little stir if separation occurs.

36.   Parsnip-Kale-Tomato

Ingredients
5 Kale Leaves
2 Parsnips
1 Tomato
2 Celery Stalks
1 Apple (or more for desired sweetness)

Directions
Throw all of the ingredients into your high-speed blender and blast for 30 to 60 seconds until well combined. Enjoy right away while still fresh, and give a little stir if separation occurs.

37.   Fabulous Fruity

Ingredients
2 apples
2 pears
2 kiwi fruit
2 oranges
1 lemon
And a handful of mint leaves
Served with ice cubes

It's a thirst quencher and cleanser so refreshing for summer, it's sweet with a citrus bite.

38.   Fruity Fast

Ingredients
Juice together:
1 Red Apple
1 Bosc Pear
1 C Carrots
1/2 Papaya
1 Bunch Spinach
1 Blood Orange

Transfer to blender add 1/2 bunch Wheatgrass
Makes two (2) 5oz glasses for my husband and I.

39.   Gorgeous Greens

Ingredients
7 stalks kale
1 apple
2 hand full spinach
1 pear
5 stalks celery

Directions
Juice kale & spinach between fruits

40.   Cute Celery

Ingredients:
1/2 cucumber
2 sticks of celery
1 orange
1 handful of baby spinach
1/2 green bell pepper
3 leaves of kail
1 tomato
2 carrots

Directions
Throw all of the ingredients into your high-speed blender and blast for 30 to 60 seconds until well combined. Enjoy right away while still fresh, and give a little stir if separation occurs.

41.   Hot and Spicy

Ingredients
Large bunch Kale (10-12 leaves)
1 Small Beet plus greens
1 Medium Watermelon Radish
2 hot peppers (or to taste)
3 large cucumbers
head of celery (5-6 stalks)
2 apples
clove garlic
1 shallot or 2 scallions
1/2 cup cilantro
whole lemon
whole lime
5-8 ripe tomatoes (if your juicer will take them, use early girl or similar, otherwise, use plum tomatoes)
1 inch of ginger (optional, I put it in all my juices)

Makes a 2 quart pitcher full, I like to put some black pepper on top as well.
Flavors reminiscent of tacos or empanadas

42.   **Cinnamon Coconut Surprise**

Ingredients
1/2 Cup Coconut Milk
4 Large Egg Yolks
1 Medium Banana
1/4 Cup Ice
1/2 tsp Cinnamon

Directions
Throw all of the ingredients into your high-speed blender and blast for 30 to 60 seconds until well combined. Enjoy right away while still fresh, and give a little stir if separation occurs.

43. Blushing Blue

Ingrdients
½ Cup Water
3 TBSP Avocado
1 Cup Blueberries, Frozen
2 Cups Spinach

Directions
Throw all of the ingredients into your high-speed blender and blast for 30 to 60 seconds until well combined. Enjoy right away while still fresh, and give a little stir if separation occurs.

44.   Blushing Banana

Ingredients
½ Cup Water
1 Medium Banana
10 Large Radish, Sliced
¼ Cup Ice

Directions
Throw all of the ingredients into your high-speed blender and blast for 30 to 60 seconds until well combined. Enjoy right away while still fresh, and give a little stir if separation occurs.

45.   Baby Kale Pineapple

Ingredients:
1 cup almond milk
1/2 cup frozen pineapple
1 cup Kale
1 tablespoon hemp protein powder

Instructions:
Place the almond milk, pineapple, and greens in the juicer.

46.   Divine Peach Coconut Juice

Ingredients:
1 cup full fat coconut milk, chilled
1 cup ice
2 large fresh peaches, peeled and cut into chunks
Fresh lemon zest, to taste
1 tablespoon hemp protein powder

Instructions:
Add coconut milk, ice and peaches blender. Using a zester, add a few gratings of fresh lemon zest.
Blend on high speed

47.   Tantalizing Key Lime Pie Juice

Ingredients:
1 cup coconut milk
1 cup ice
1/2 avocado
zest and juice of 2 limes
Pure liquid stevia to taste
1 tablespoon hemp protein powder

Instructions:
Add all ingredients to Vitamix or blender and blend.

48.   High Protein and Nutritional Delish

Ingredients:

1 cup almond milk

1/2 Avocado

4 Strawberries

1/2 Bananas (Very ripe)

1/2 cup Raw Kale or spinach

1/4 cup Carrot Juice) water can be used

1 cup Coconut Yogurt. or almond milk)

1 tablespoon hemp protein powder

Instructions: Add everything to your blender, and blend to your preferred consistency. More water or ice can be added.

49.   Ginger Carrot Protein Juice

Ingredients:

3/4 cup carrot juice

1 tablespoon hemp protein powder

1 tablespoon hulled hemp seeds

1/2 apple

3 to 4 ice cubes

1/2 inch piece fresh ginger

Instructions:

Add to a blender and blend.

50.   Green Juice

1 – I start with 3/4 to 1 cup of water.

2 – Then I choose three vegetables. Typically, I use about 3 cups or large handfuls of spinach, one whole carrot and one or two small vine tomatoes.

3 – Next, I choose three fruits. I start with either mango, pear or apple for the base, then I add one whole orange and either 1 cup blueberries, strawberries or pineapple to flavor.

4 – Sometimes, I will add about 1/4-1/3 avocado which helps give the smoothie a nice creamy texture while boosting the calories and healthy fat content to make the smoothie more satisfying.

5 – Start by adding the liquid to your blender (see my blender recommendations), followed by the soft fruit. Add the greens to your blender last. Blend on high for 30 seconds.

Chapter 4:

Juicing Your Fat Away

Synopsis

Incorporating the juicing exercise into a weight loss diet plan is a very effective way to shed the weight. However it should be noted that the juicing process should ideally include both vegetables and fruits as concentrating on only fruits will not be beneficial because most fruits usually have high sugar contents.

Get The Fat Out

Juicing is also a good ingredient for any detoxifying exercise and it can be used as a meal replacement or when there is a fasting plan in place. If the juicing purpose is meant to detoxify, then it will function to push out all the toxins and fats that have accumulated over time in the body system.

These juices will work as cleansing agents which would be an ideal substitute to a heavy unhealthy meal. Juicing will also be a more healthy and realistic way to lose weight.

Most juicing recipes that are designed for weight loss are very nutritious and satisfying to ensure the individual does not have to resort to supplementing it with other food items due to hunger pangs.

They also usually include ingredients that are specifically part of the combination for the characteristics of sweeping away the toxins and fats.

It is also recommended to ensure that all the ingredients used in the juicing recipes are fresh produce and it should all be cleaned thoroughly before actually commencing the juicing exercise.

The following are some recopies that would serve well in the quest to juicing the fat away:

Apple berry fiber – the apples are excellent cleansing agents while the berries provide the mineral supplements.

Green pineapple – this concoction is simply refreshing and bursting with goodness and also feels very filling.

Orange pineapple chilli – being full of vitamin C, and having enzymes that can dissolve mucus accumulated in the body, it also speeds up the metabolic system.

Gingered pear – a great laxative option and good for digestion.

JUST JUICE By Danielle James

Chapter 5:

Juicing For Kids

Synopsis

Most times it is a struggle for both parents and children when it comes to tackling the issue of eating vegetables and fruits served at meals. However with the discovery of juicing this problem for most has been eradicated or at the very least decreased to controllable levels.

For The Little Ones

Juicing is a great and fun way to get nutrition into the bodies of growing children to ensure optimal development of their bodies. The trick is to design concoctions that are pleasant to drink and are also refreshing especially after a strenuous playing session.

However for younger children it would be advisable to dilute the juices, as the concentrated form may be too much for the underdeveloped body to deal with.

Teenagers and older kids should have to problems with drinking concentrated juices. Introducing juices to kids should be done in a gradual process with initial stages of diluting.

Choosing fruits that have delectable tastes is much better and less likely to be rejected by the child. Starting out with single juice choices before moving on the combinations is also advised, as this will allow the body system and the child's palate to get used to this introduction into the healthy daily diet plan.

Changing the juices and providing a variety is definitely an attractive feature for children and they would be fascinated with the colors and tastes reflected in the variety.

Once the favorite juices are identified, serving them as often as possible without boring the child will be beneficial. Using the favorite juice as a base, it may also be possible to add on a little portion of other fruits or vegetables to further enhance the nutrient content of the juice.

Some popular choices may include apple juice, pineapple and carrot juice, orange juice, orange and carrot juice pear juice and apple and grape juice.

JUST JUICE By Danielle James

Chapter 6:

Juicing For Anti-aging

Synopsis

Juicing is not the new fad to combat natural aging processes. If makes sense to opt for this healthier and cheaper yet no less effective way of starving off the aging process.

Staying Younger

Juicing benefits the body as it provides the combination of all the essential vitamins, minerals, amino acids, essential fatty acids, and enzymes.

These fruits and vegetable that are usually used in the juicing process are also power packed with anti aging and life preserving elements, thus the choice made to incorporate regular juicing exercises would benefit greatly.

The antioxidants and substances that neutralize the free radicals in the system ideally provide the possibility of having good anti aging benefits.

A diet rich with vitamins and minerals is the key factor to fighting against the aging process and one of the most pleasant ways of doing this is through the juicing exercise.

Brightly colored fruits and vegetables are especially beneficial for the anti aging fight. Fruits such as oranges, cherries, tangerines, apples, blueberries, cranberries, melons, bananas, grapes, berries, kiwi, and mangoes are all know for the anti aging properties.

These can be taken in combinations or separately, whichever is suitable for the individual's palate. When it comes to vegetable there is the abundant choice of carrots, squash, red and green cabbages, broccoli, spinach which are just as beneficial for their anti aging properties too.

Apple carrot detox – 1 apple, 1 slice of ginger, 1 carrot, ½ cup or water. Its excellent properties that creates healthy skin and eliminates toxin form the body is the reason this juice is a popular choice for many.

Cholesterol burner – 1 apple, ½ cucumber, 4 stalks of celery, ½ cup of water. This juice is a good controller of high cholesterol levels in the body system and also helps to fight against upset stomachs, besides the more obvious anti aging properties it carries.

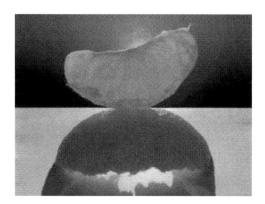

JUST JUICE By Danielle James

Chapter 7:

Juicing For Detoxification

Synopsis

The juicing process is ideal for detoxification of the body system, as it enhances the enzymes, vitamins and mineral absorption which in turn greatly benefits the immune system.

Detox

Juicing organic vegetables and fruits which are rich in nutrients will help to cover the cells in the body with the alkaline juices released from these juicing concoctions whereby acids are released and toxins can be removed through various elimination channels in the body.

The parts of the body that play an important role in filtering such toxins would include the lungs, kidneys, skin and other functions like urinary and bowel movements.

The enzymes released from these juices also help the digestive processed where the proteins break down the foods into nutrients and this is an important function as most adults have already used up their natural digestive enzymes by the age of 30.

Therefore the outside aid that the juices provide is definitely beneficial to the digestive process as it is pivotal in the detoxifying regiment the body naturally enlists.

When the body is full of toxins it is unable to absorb the nutrients that are available in the natural intake of regular foods, thus the need for these added juices to assist in the breakdown of the toxins to cleanse the body and carry the appropriate amount to oxygen and nutrients directly to the cell and tissues.

Some of the ideal ingredients to use in the juicing process for detoxifying would include lettuce, dark green kale, carrots, beet greens, cilantro, parsley, celery sticks, collard greens, endive, spinach, dandelion greens, cabbage both purple and green and lemons.

Some people who practice this detoxifying regiment periodically attest to the fact that they no longer have cravings for sweetened foods and they can keep to a regular and healthy diet without any struggles. This is probably due to the fact that the body is able to function at its optimum because of the detoxifying sessions.

JUST JUICE By Danielle James

Chapter 8:

Social Marketing

Synopsis

It has already been established that juicing is a very healthy exercise to practice. This is also one of the contributing factors that ensure the individual's chances of developing any medical problems are considerably lessened. By lowering the risk of having diseases the juicing habit has proven to be one that everyone should consider for its merits.

Staying Healthy

There are several very specific combinations that can be used regularly of create the ideal effects within the body system that allow it to resist any possible occurrences of diseases.

One of which, is drinking a beetroot combination, as this is said to dramatically reduce the risks of heart disease, strokes, Alzheimer's and dementia.

The bright red juice contains the chemical nitrate which dramatically reduces blood pressure for almost everyone taking this remedy.

Another juice combination is the one with pomegranate content which is pivotal in lowering cardiovascular risks, however this should be taken with care as the potassium content is rather high. Tomato juice combinations are also supposed to help lower heart diseases and control diabetic symptoms.

Other benefits from consuming tomato juice would include the resistance to developing chronic diseases like cancer and coronary heart disease. This can be avoided because of the carotenoid content called lycopene which is richly found in tomatoes.

Some of the ingredients that can be used to combat or at least lower the risks of diseases would include broccoli, Brussels sprouts, butter squash, cabbage, Chinese broccoli, kale, spinach, parsley, collards greens, mustards green, chard, beetroot, carrots, cauliflower, cucumber, green pepper, sweet potatoes, lettuce and celery.

Regular combinations of these juices will help to keep the chemical balance in the body system which in turn will allow the body to perform at its prime thus effectively avoiding any diseases.

JUST JUICE By Danielle James

Chapter 9:

Juicing For Stress Relieving

Synopsis

Almost everyone adult and child alike has experienced bouts of stress at various points in their daily life. For most, this is taken in stride until it is no longer possible to do so, and when this happens it almost always affects the health conditions.

Destress

Fruit and vegetable juices have long been known for their stress relief and relaxation properties. Therefore taking the time to explore this healthy alternative to popping pill to relieve stress is certainly worth the effort.

Apple, cherry and blueberry ingredients have been known to be good health boosting elements where the flavonoid can facilitate better lung functions and with this optimum breathing position the ideal amounts of oxygen is then able to be circulated well with the body system thus relieving any internal pressures felt when stress levels are high and this eventually helps to lower the stress levels.

These ingredients can also contribute to relaxing the arteries and lowering the risk of cardiovascular diseases which are often caused by stress. Smoothies made from bananas, strawberry, peppermint and lemon can all help to relieve stress and create the relaxing overall body feeling.

When the adrenaline levels increase the body requires more vitamin C and as this cannot be naturally conjured by the human body there is a need to have this supplemented for outside sources, thus the advantage of the afore mentioned ingredients.

Bananas would contribute to stress relief properties while the peppermint which contains menthol will have a cooling effect on the body while the others will help in digestion, thus creating an overall effect that will combat any significant presence of stress.

JUST JUICE By Danielle James

Wrapping Up

New discoveries have shown consuming fruits and vegetables, in the form of juices have been able to show significant benefits to the body system when ingested in regular intervals.

FREE GIFT

27 Smoothie Recipes

Smoothies

1. Gorgeous Berry Smoothie

Ingredients:
½ cup frozen blueberries or 1 cup fresh blueberries
15 oz coconut milk
Stevia to taste
1 scoop of hemp protein
¼ teaspoon cinnamon (optional)

Instructions:
Place all ingredients into a blender.

Blend until mixed thoroughly.

Serve right away.

2. *Tempting Coconut Berry Smoothie*

Ingredients:
½ Cup Frozen Blackberries
½ Frozen Banana
1 Teaspoon Chia Seeds
¼ Inch Piece of Fresh Ginger
½ Cup Almond
Coconut Milk
1 scoop of HEMP protein
2 Tablespoons Toasted Coconut

Instructions:
Combine all the ingredients in a blender and process until smooth.

3. *Volumptious Vanilla Hot Drink*

Ingredients:
3 cups unsweetened almond milk (or 1 1/2 cup full fat coconut milk +
1 1/2 cups
water)
Stevia to taste
1 scoop of hemp protein
1/2 Tbsp. ground cinnamon (or more to taste)
1/2 Tbsp. vanilla extract

Instructions:
Place the almond milk into a pitcher. Place ground cinnamon, hemp, anilla extract in a small saucepan over medium high heat. Heat until the pure liquid stevia is just melted and then pour the pure liquid stevia mixture into the pitcher.

Stir until the pure liquid stevia is well combined with the almond milk. Place the pitcher in the fridge and allow to chill for at least two hours. Stir well before serving.

4. Almond Butter Smoothies

Ingredients:
1 scoop of hemp protein
1 Tablespoon natural almond butter
1 cup of hemp milk
1 banana, preferably frozen for a creamier shake
few ice cubes

Instructions:
Blend all ingredients together and enjoy!

5. Choco Walnut Delight

Ingredients:
1 scoop Hemp Protein
30g dark sugar free chocolate broken up.
50g walnuts chopped/crushed (depending on desired texture)
250ml hemp milk or nut milk alternative
Handfull of ice cubes, the more you use the thicker it will be.

Instructions:
Blend everything together in a strong blender until thoroughly processed, and enjoy!

Makes 2, and can be stored in the fridge overnight.

6. Raspberry Hemp Smoothie

Ingredients:
1 cup hemp milk or milk alternative.
1/2 cup raspberries (fresh or frozen)
2 tablespoons hemp protein powder
Stevia to taste
3 to 4 ice cubes

Instructions:
Add ingredients to a blender and blend until smooth.

7. *Choco Banana Smoothie*

Ingredients:
1 cup milk or milk alternative
2 peeled frozen bananas
4 ice cubes
2 tablespoons hulled hemp seed
2 tablespoons hemp protein powder
1 tablespoons organic cocoa powder
5-7 drops liquid stevia to sweeten
1/4 teaspoon cinnamon
1/4 teaspoon vanilla

Instructions:
Put all ingredients into blender. Blend until smooth.

8. *Blueberry Almond Smoothie*

Ingredients:
1 c almond milk
1 c frozen unsweetened blueberries
1 Tbsp cold-pressed organic flaxseed oil
2 tblsp hemp protein powder

Instructions:
Combine milk and blueberries in blender, and blend for 1 minute.

Transfer to glass, and stir in flaxseed oil.

9. *Hazelnut Butter and Banana Smoothie*

Ingredients:
½ c nut milk
½ c hemp milk
2 Tbsp creamy natural unsalted hazelnut butter
¼ very ripe banana stevia drops to taste
4 ice cubes
2 tblsp hemp protein powder

Instructions:
Combine ingredients in a blender. Process until smooth.

Pour into a tall glass and serve.

10. *Vanilla Blueberry Smoothie*

Ingredients:
2 cups hemp milk
1 c fresh blueberries
Handful of ice OR 1 cup frozen blueberries
1 Tbsp flaxseed oil
2 tblsp hemp protein powder

Instructions:
Combine milk, and fresh blueberries plus ice (or frozen blueberries) in a blender.

Blend for 1 minute, transfer to a glass, and stir in flaxseed oil.

11. *Chocolate Raspberry Smoothie*

Ingredients:
1 cup almond milk
¼ c chocolate chips-sugar free
1 c fresh raspberries
2 tsp hemp protein powder
Handful of ice OR 1 cup frozen raspberries

Instructions:
COMBINE ingredients in a blender.

Blend for 1 minute, transfer to a glass, and eat with a spoon.

12. *Peach Smoothie*

Ingredients:
1 cup hemp milk
1 c frozen unsweetened peaches
2 tsp cold-pressed organic flaxseed oil (MUFA)
2 tsp hemp protein powder

Instructions:
PLACE milk and frozen, unsweetened peaches in blender and blend for 1 minute.

Transfer to glass, and stir in flaxseed oil.

13. *Zesty Citrus Smoothie*

Ingredients:
1 cup almond milk
half cup lemon juice
1 med orange peeled, cleaned, and sliced into sections
Handful of ice
1 Tbsp flaxseed oil
2 tsp hemp protein powder

Instructions:
COMBINE milk, lemon juice, orange, and ice in a blender.

Blend for 1 minute, transfer to a glass, and stir in flaxseed oil.

14. *Apple Smoothie*

Ingredients:
½ cup hemp milk
1 cup hemp milk
1 tsp apple pie spice
1 med apple peeled and chopped
2 Tbsp cashew butter
Handful of ice
2 tblsp hemp protein powder

Instructions:
COMBINE ingredients in a blender.

Blend for 1 minute, transfer to a glass, and eat with a spoon.

15. *Pineapple Smoothie*

Ingredients:
1 cup almond milk
4 oz fresh pineapple
Handful of ice
2 tblsp hemp protein powder
1 Tbsp cold-pressed organic flaxseed oil

Instructions:
PLACE milk, canned pineapple in blender, add of ice, and whip for 1 minute.

Transfer to glass and stir in flaxseed oil.

16. *Strawberry Smoothie*

Ingredients:
1 cup almond milk
1 c frozen, unsweetened strawberries
2 tblsp hemp protein powder
2 tsp cold-pressed organic flaxseed oil

Instructions:
COMBINE milk and strawberries in blender.

Blend, transfer to glass, and stir in flaxseed oil.

17. *Pineapple Coconut Deluxe Smoothie*

Ingredients:
1 C pineapple chunks
1 C coconut milk
1/2 C pineapple juice
1 ripe banana
1/2 – 3/4 C ice cubes
Pure liquid stevia to taste
1 tablespoon hemp protein powder

Instructions:
In a blender, combine the pineapple chunks, coconut milk, banana, ice and pure liquid stevia.

Puree until smooth.

Pour into 2 large glasses.

Garnish with a pineapple wedge if desired.

18. Divine Vanilla Smoothie

Ingredients:
1 cup coconut or almond milk
¼ cup almond butter
1 tsp vanilla paste, (or vanilla extract)
2 cups ice
Vanilla liquid, seeds or powder, to taste
Vanilla or plain hemp Protein Powder – 1 tablespoon

Instructions:
Add all ingredients except ice to blender. Puree well.

Add ice and blend until ice is all crushed and smoothie is well blended and smooth.

Pour into two glasses and serve immediately.

NOTES
Add more or less ice to make the smoothie thinner or thicker consistency.
Great for a post workout smoothie!

19. Coco Orange Delish Smoothie

Ingredients:
1/2 cup fresh squeezed orange juice (I used 1 1/2 oranges)
1 tablespoon hemp protein powder
1/2 cup full fat coconut milk from the can (not the box!)
1 teaspoon vanilla
1/2 -1 cup crushed ice

Instructions:
Add all ingredients to a blender.

Blend until smooth and add ice as needed to get the consistency you like.

20. Baby Kale Pineapple Smoothie

Ingredients:
1 cup almond milk
1/2 cup frozen pineapple
1 cup Kale
1 tablespoon hemp protein powder

Instructions:
Place the almond milk, pineapple, and greens in the blender and blend until smooth.

21. *Sumptuous Strawberry Coconut Smoothie*

Ingredients:
1 cup coconut milk
1 frozen banana, sliced
2 cups frozen strawberries
1 teaspoon vanilla extract
1 tablespoon hemp protein powder

Instructions:
Add all ingredients to blender and blend until smooth.

22. *Blueberry Bonanza Smoothies*

Ingredients:
1/4 cup canned coconut or almond milk
1/2 cup water
1 medium banana, sliced
1 cup frozen blueberries
1 tablespoon raw almonds

Instructions:
Add coconut milk, water, banana, blueberries and almonds to blender container.

Cover and blend until smooth. Pour into 2 glasses.

23. *Divine Peach Coconut Smoothie*

Ingredients:
1 cup full fat coconut milk, chilled
1 cup ice
2 large fresh peaches, peeled and cut into chunks
Fresh lemon zest, to taste
1 tablespoon hemp protein powder

Instructions:
Add coconut milk, ice and peaches blender. Using a zester, add a few gratings of fresh lemon zest.

Blend on high speed until smooth.

24. Tantalizing Key Lime Pie Smoothie

Ingredients:
1 cup coconut milk
1 cup ice
1/2 avocado
zest and juice of 2 limes
Pure liquid stevia to taste
1 tablespoon hemp protein powder

Instructions:
Add all ingredients to Vitamix or blender and blend until smooth.

25. *High Protein and Nutritional Delish Smoothie*

Ingredients:
1 cup almond milk
1/2 Avocado
4 Strawberries
1/2 Bananas (Very ripe)
1/2 cup Raw Kale or spinach
1/4 cup Carrot Juice) water can be used
1 cup Coconut Yogurt..or almond milk)
1 tablespoon hemp protein powder

Instructions:
Add everything to your blender, and blend to your preferred consistency

More water or ice can be added to help with your preferred texture/thickness.

26. Pineapple Protein Smoothie

Ingredients:
1 cup (135g) pineapple chunks
1 cup (200g) coconut milk (fresh or tinned)
½ med (65g) banana
¼ cup (65g) ice cubes
¼ tsp vanilla bean powder
pinch low sodium salt
1 tablespoon hemp protein powder

Instructions:
Peel pineapple and chop into small chunks.

Put everything into a high speed blender and blend until smooth.

27. Raspberry Coconut Smoothie

Ingredients:
½ - 1 cup coconut milk (depending on how thick you like it)
1 medium banana, peeled sliced and frozen
2 teaspoons coconut extract (optional)
1 cup frozen raspberries
1 tablespoon hemp protein powder

optional: shredded coconut flakes, and stevia to taste

Instructions:
Add coconut milk, frozen banana slices and coconut extract to your blender.

Pulse 1-2 minutes until smooth.

Add frozen raspberries and continue to pulse until smooth.

Pour into your serving glass, top with a couple of raspberries and a little shredded coconut, and enjoy!

JUST JUICE By Danielle James

AUTHOR BIOGRAPHY

Hi! I'm Danielle James and it's a real pleasure to be working with you. My books are all about helping you to lose weight, to get in great shape and discover whole new ways to feel stronger and fitter than you've ever felt before. Helping people in this way is the driving source of my motivation and making a positive, measurable difference to my readers is my personal mission. That's what gets me up in the mornings with a smile on my face!

You might think I've been incredibly lucky but my life wasn't always about being super-fit and full of natural energy. Let me tell you right off the bat that I've had more than my fair share of problems with weight gain and yo-yo dieting! So I know exactly what it feels like to carry a lot of extra weight and how frustrating it can be to try to lose it.

To understand how my problems developed, we need to go back to my childhood for a moment. I grew up in the seventies in the beautiful mid-West of America, one of four kids with loving parents in a close-knit family and a very stable childhood. So, in that sense, I was truly blessed and very fortunate, but I guess I first started to pile on weight during my high school years. We were all a lot more active as kids in those days but we sure ate a lot too – including the inevitable junk food - and my weight gain was mostly laughed off as a natural product of adolescence. But the weight persisted into my college years and I began to worry that it might've become a permanent feature of my life. Sure, I wasn't the only gal with a bunch of extra pounds around the middle but I felt pretty self-conscious about my weight and that's when I started to experiment with diets.

Over the past twenty years or so, I must've tried every diet and food fad that's ever been marketed. You name it and I've probably tried it. But, like so many people today who are desperate to get their weight under control, I was constantly frustrated by the short-term effects of dieting. Sure, I'd lose a few pounds here and there but they always came back with a vengeance.

Settling down and having a family of my own only made the weight issues more acute and I began to experience minor health problems too, embarrassing reactions including eczema and rashes, chronic bloating and fatigue. My doctor prescribed a steroid treatment to control the skin problems but we both knew we were only treating the symptoms rather than the underlying cause of the problems.

That was when I came across an on-line article on the Paleo diet, written by a highly respected nutritionist, who claimed that this was the absolute best way to tackle weight issues and the long list of harmful problems that result from our modern diet. To be honest, I didn't feel I had anything to lose. Over the years since college, I'd tried everything else to lose weight but the article made a lot of sense to me and the research behind the diet was impressive. So I made a decision to try this new eating style and I bet you can guess the result, can't you? That's right. The pounds fell away, my skin issues cleared up one hundred percent, my energy levels soared and I started to feel better than I had since I was a kid! Impressed? My husband suddenly noticed that he was married to a 'hottie' and everyone wanted to know why I was looking so much younger, fitter, healthier and, in all truth, a darn sight happier. Changing your food choices can have the most far-reaching effects imaginable on your health and wellbeing and that became my motivation to study to become a nutritionist.

That simple yet profound decision formed the basis for my new career and I've been privileged to work with groups and individuals across the country, advising on the benefits of the Paleo approach and receiving fan mail from very happy people in more than seventy countries around the world. The improvements in the quality of people's lives has to be experienced to be believed but it's become my mission in life to spread the knowledge about this remarkable way of healing the body, burning off the unwanted fat and discovering the joy of a healthy body wherever I can.

I'm delighted to welcome you to the growing band of wonderful people who are living such a different life today because of the power of this amazing way of fuelling and nourishing the body. Enjoy the results – you only deserve the best!

Before You Go.......

Thank you again for choosing this book and for reading it through to the end. We really hope you enjoyed the contents and that's why we appreciate your feedback so much.

If you could take a couple of minutes to review the book, your views will help us to focus on the material that you want to read.
Let us know how we can help and thank you for your support and encouragement.

MORE SIMILAR BOOKS

100 Best PALEO Soup, Smoothie & Juice Recipes

Please search this page over the internet
www.amazon.com/s/ref=nb_sb_noss?url=search-
alias%3Dstripbooks&field-keywords=B01KX5Z46Q

The best way to take control of your weight, naturally, easily and with fabulously delicious recipes.

Powerful, effective and a simply delicious approach to losing weight the way Nature intended. Recommended by doctors, nutritionists and healthcare professionals, this master class in smart nutrition is your daily meal planner and life-changing cook book.

Paleo Cookbook: The New PALEO PKE Recipe Book (250 of the Best Paleo-Keto-Epigenetic Recipes): Transform your Weight Loss into a Feast for the Taste-buds!

Please search this page over the internet
www.amazon.com/gp/product/B013EZAZO8?ie=UTF8&camp=1789&
creativeASIN=B013EZAZO8&linkCode=xm2&tag=onelifeblog-20

Put the power of natural rejuvenation into your body with the smartest nutrition and anti-ageing methods available today.

Taming the tides of time with the latest research in rejuvenation techniques, this is the intelligent way to fuel the body and restore youthful vitality from the inside. Filled with delicious, nutritious and highly effective recipes, this is a superb companion volume to the original Paleo Epigenetic Bible.

Paleo Recipe Book: The Fifty, Fit and Fabulous Anti-Ageing PALEO Cookbook.(Blissful Flavours for Ageless Vitality): Stay Slim with 250 ANTI-AGEING Recipes ... Experience a World of Incredible Flavour Kindle

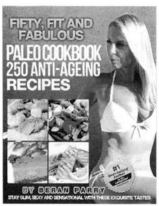

Please search this page over the internet
www.amazon.com/gp/product/B014VR2YQA?ie=UTF8&camp=1789&
creativeASIN=B014VR2YQA&linkCode=xm2&tag=onelifeblog-20

JUST JUICE By Danielle James

The essential guide to losing weight and feeling super energised with the smartest, most natural nutrition.

Feeling incredibly well and full of energy is not a matter of chance. These are the natural results of using intelligent nutrition to free your body from a lifetime of toxins, pollutants and inflammatory agents. International expert and leading specialist in smart nutrition and total wellbeing, Beran Parry leads the way in sharing the most effective ways to harness your potential for absolute health and a leaner, skinnier body.

Smart Diets: 101 Essential Habits for a Leaner New YOU (Find Your Real Body): Lose Your Weight Intelligently (Feel Fantastic) Rejuvenate and Energise

Please search this page over the internet
www.amazon.com/s/ref=nb_sb_noss?url=search-alias%3Ddigital-text&field-keywords=B00Z9WMUNO

9664395R00076

Printed in Germany
by Amazon Distribution
GmbH, Leipzig